D0115599

Spiritual Gifts

BIBLE STUDY GUIDE

From the Bible-teaching ministry of

Charles R. Swindoll

INSIGHT FOR LIVING

Charles R. Swindoll is a graduate of Dallas Theological Seminary and has served in pastorates for more than twenty-three years, including churches in Texas, New England, and California. Since 1971 he has served as senior pastor of the First Evangelical Free Church of Fullerton, California. Chuck's radio program, "Insight for Living," began in 1979. In addition to his church and radio ministries, Chuck has authored twenty-one books and numerous booklets on a variety of subjects.

Based on the outlines of Chuck's sermons, the study guide text is coauthored by Ken Gire, Jr., a graduate of Texas Christian University and Dallas Theological Seminary. The Living Insights are written by Bill Butterworth, a graduate of Florida Bible College, Dallas Theological Seminary, and Florida Atlantic University. Ken Gire, Jr., is presently the director of educational products at Insight for Living, and Bill Butterworth is currently the director of counseling ministries.

Editor in Chief:	Cynthia Swindoll
Coauthor of Text:	Ken Gire, Jr.
Author of Living Insights:	Bill Butterworth
Editorial Assistant:	Karene Wells
Copy Manager:	Jac La Tour
Senior Copy Assistant:	Jane Gillis
Copy Assistant:	Delia Gomez
Director, Communications Division:	Carla Beck
Project Manager:	Nina Paris
Art Director:	Becky Englund
Production Artists:	Kathi Hilaski and Donna Mayo
Typographer:	Bob Haskins
Calligrapher:	David Acquistapace
Cover Photograph:	FourByFive
Print Production Manager:	Deedee Snyder
Printer:	Frye and Smith

Unless otherwise identified, all Scripture references are from the New American Standard Bible, © The Lockman Foundation 1960, 1962, 1963, 1968, 1971, 1972, 1973, 1975, 1977. Used by permission.

© 1972, 1978, 1980, 1983, 1986 by Charles R. Swindoll. All rights reserved. Printed in the United States of America. No portion of this publication may be reproduced in any form, except for brief quotations in reviews, without prior written permission of the publisher, Insight for Living, Post Office Box 4444, Fullerton, California 92634.

ISBN 0-8499-8291-X

Ordering Information

An album that contains six messages on three cassettes and corresponds to this study guide may be purchased through Insight for Living, Post Office Box 4444, Fullerton, California 92634. For ordering information and a current catalog, please write our office or call (714) 870-9161.

Canadian residents may obtain a catalog and ordering information through Insight for Living Ministries, Post Office Box 2510, Vancouver, British Columbia, Canada V6B 3W7, (604) 272-5811. Overseas residents should direct their correspondence to our Fullerton office.

If you wish to order by Visa or MasterCard, you are welcome to use our toll-free number, (800) 772-8888, Monday through Friday between the hours of 8:30 A.M. and 4:00 P.M., Pacific time. This number may be used anywhere in the continental United States excluding Alaska, California, and Hawaii. Orders from those areas can be made by calling our general office number, (714) 870-9161. Orders from Canada can be made by calling (604) 272-5811.

Table of Contents

Spiritual Gifts

The orchestration of the Body is something beautiful to behold. Christ Himself selects who will play each instrument. As the conductor, He determines the sections and then decides which parts each will play. Because He is also the composer, the music He writes is perfectly designed to impact the world as well as encourage the members of the orchestra. It's a phenomenon duplicated nowhere else.

Did you know that as a child of God, you are a member of this vast orchestra? Were you aware that the Lord has placed instruments in your hands that play a vital part in His composition? Those instruments are called "spiritual gifts" in the New Testament. I exhort you to cultivate your gifts so you can play your part in His phenomenal plan.

I hope these studies will help you discover your gifts and the value of your contribution. What beautiful music we can make together!

Chuck Swindoll

Putting Truth into Action

Knowledge apart from application falls short of God's desire for His children. Knowledge must result in change and growth. Consequently, we have constructed this Bible study guide with these purposes in mind: (1) to stimulate discovery, (2) to increase understanding, and (3) to encourage application.

At the end of each lesson is a section called 🖫 *Living Insights.* There you'll be given assistance in further Bible study, thoughtful interaction, and personal appropriation. This is the place where the lesson is fitted with shoe leather for your walk through the varied experiences of life.

It's our hope that you'll discover numerous ways to use this tool. Some useful avenues we would suggest are personal meditation, joint discovery, and discussion with your spouse, family, work associates, friends, or neighbors. The study guide is also practical for church classes and, of course, as a study aid for the "Insight for Living" radio broadcast.

In order to derive the greatest benefit from this process, we suggest that you record your responses to the lessons in a notebook where writing space is plentiful. In view of the kinds of questions asked, your notebook may become a journal filled with your many discoveries and commitments. We anticipate that you will find yourself returning to it periodically for review and encouragement.

Ken Gire, Jr.
Coauthor of Text

Bill Butterworth
Author of Living Insights

Spiritual Gifts

Spiritual Gifts in a Spiritual Body

1 Corinthians 12:1–11

Memories of Christmas warm us like a handmade quilt on a December morning: the rustic manger scene enticing little eyes and little hands ... eagerly hung, oversized stockings ... steal-a-kiss mistletoe ... glazed porcelain mugs steaming wraithlike wisps of hot spiced cider into the air, mingling with the ubiquitous scent of pine ... caravans of colored lights entwining themselves around the tree ... a hodgepodge of festive ornaments. And presents, lots of presents wrapped and waiting, handpicked by the parents for each child—a cuddly stuffed animal for one, a model airplane for another, a baby doll, a football—all waiting patiently under the tree for Christmas morning.

So much thought and emotion goes into picking each gift. Imagine how hurt you would be if, after picking just the right gifts, beautifully wrapping each one, placing them under the tree, and giving them out on Christmas morning, they were received with indifference. How would you feel if your children simply took them—without acknowledgment, without thanks, without even bothering to open them—and then casually laid them aside?

Now imagine how the Lord must feel when He gives gifts to His children, and they never take the trouble to find out what the gifts are, never thank Him, never put them to use.

Shelved away, never to be shared—that's where most spiritual gifts end up. In this study on spiritual gifts, we're going to change all that. We're going to take those gifts out of mothballs, unwrap them one by one, and put them into action. Like a wide-eyed child in pajamas on Christmas morning, you're in for a special treat! In this lesson, before we actually discuss individual gifts, we'll spend some time answering questions which may have puzzled you concerning spiritual gifts.

I. What Is a Spiritual Gift?

Within 1 Corinthians 12 the term *gifts* appears six times (vv. 1, 4, 9, 28, 30, 31). The first usage varies from the others in that the word *gifts*

1

does not actually appear in the original Greek:[1] "Now concerning spiritual gifts, brethren, I do not want you to be unaware" (v. 1). Literally, the text reads: "Now concerning spirituals..." or "Now concerning spiritual things..." Translators have supplied the word *gifts* because that is the thrust of the passage. In the other instances, the word *gifts* is a rendering of the Greek *charisma*.[2] The root of this word is *charis,* meaning "grace." Grace is commonly defined as "unmerited favor"—God giving us something we don't deserve and can't earn. Therefore, we conclude that spiritual gifts are given to us as an unmerited gift from God. William McRae defines a gift as follows:

> As to its essence, a spiritual gift is an ability. It is an ability to function effectively and significantly in a particular service as a member of Christ's body, the church.[3]

Spiritual gifts should be distinguished from natural gifts, which are particular artistic, athletic, or mental abilities or talents. Natural gifts are given to us at birth, ultimately by God but genetically inherited from our parents. Spiritual gifts are given to us at conversion, at our new birth. They are given by God, independent of our parents.[4]

┌─ A Thought to Consider ───────────

Like a parent giving gifts at Christmas, when God gives spiritual gifts, He *stoops* to give them. He distributes gifts, not because we merit them, but because He is such a good and gracious giver (James 1:17).

II. Is There a Difference between the Gift of the Holy Spirit and Spiritual Gifts?

The gift of the Holy Spirit and spiritual gifts are definitely different. The first is singular; the second, plural. The first is the Holy Spirit Himself; the second is the gifts which He imparts. In the upper room, where Christ met with His disciples shortly before His arrest and execution, He spoke of the Holy Spirit as a promised gift.

> "If you ask Me anything in My name, I will do it. If you love Me, you will keep My commandments. And I will ask the Father, and He will give you another Helper, that He may be with you forever." (John 14:14–16)

1. This is why the New American Standard Bible italicizes the word *gifts* in 1 Corinthians 12:1. The word *spiritual* is from the Greek *pneumatikos.*

2. From this ancient word we get the words *charisma* and *charismatic.*

3. William McRae, *Dynamics of Spiritual Gifts* (Grand Rapids, Mich.: Zondervan Publishing House, 1976), p. 18.

4. For a good discussion on this distinction, see the chapter titled "The Definition of a Gift" in McRae's book *Dynamics of Spiritual Gifts,* pp. 20–22.

Jesus referred to the Holy Spirit as "another Helper"[5] given by the Father not only to be *with* them but *in* them (v. 17). The promise of the Holy Spirit was emphasized by repeating the word *will* four times and was fulfilled at Pentecost.

> Now when they heard this [the truth about Jesus], they were pierced to the heart, and said to Peter and the rest of the apostles, "Brethren, what shall we do?" And Peter said to them, "Repent, and let each of you be baptized in the name of Jesus Christ for the forgiveness of your sins; and you shall receive the gift of the Holy Spirit." (Acts 2:37–38)[6]

III. Who Gives and Receives Spiritual Gifts?

Many would argue that spiritual gifts are given as a result of praying, waiting, and earnestly desiring them. But Scripture clearly teaches that the gifts are *sovereignly* given by the Holy Spirit according to God's blueprint.

> For to one is given the word of wisdom through the Spirit, and to another the word of knowledge according to the same Spirit; to another faith by the same Spirit, and to another gifts of healing by the one Spirit.... But one and the same Spirit works all these things, distributing to each one individually just as He wills.... And God has appointed in the church, first apostles, second prophets, third teachers, then miracles, then gifts of healings, helps, administrations, various kinds of tongues. (1 Cor. 12:8–9, 11, 28)

The recipients of the gifts are clearly all believers.

> For by one Spirit we were *all* baptized into one body, whether Jews or Greeks, whether slaves or free, and we were *all* made to drink of one Spirit. (v. 13, emphasis added)

---

5. The word *another* is from the Greek *allos,* meaning "another of the same kind." The word *helper* means "one called alongside to administer aid, comfort, or assistance."

6. Acts 2:38 has caused significant interpretational confusion for many commentators. The verse appears to be saying that baptism is necessary for salvation. However, the New Testament is replete with the good news that salvation comes by faith *alone* (John 1:12, 3:16; Acts 2:21; Rom. 10:9–13; Eph. 2:8–9). As we look closely at the verse, the fly in the exegetical ointment is the little preposition *for.* The tendency is to interpret it as introducing a purpose clause ("in order that"). When we say "Let's go to the barbershop for a haircut," we are using *for* in that sense. But when we say "The man was electrocuted for murder," we are using the preposition in a causal sense ("because of"). If this latter usage is meant in Acts 2:38, the apparent confusion is removed. In essence, Peter was exhorting the people to repent and be baptized *because of* the forgiveness of their sins. See also verse 41, where baptism happens because the people received the Word.

IV. Does the Bible Give a List of Spiritual Gifts for Us to Consult?

The New Testament provides us with six lists, which are charted here for easy reference. The main list is found in 1 Corinthians 12:28, where gifts are listed in the order of their importance to the body.

New Testament Lists of Spiritual Gifts		
1 Corinthians 12:8–10	1 Corinthians 12:28	1 Corinthians 12:29–30
Word of wisdom Word of knowledge Faith Healing Miracles Prophecy Distinguishing of spirits Tongues Interpretation of tongues	Apostleship Prophecy Teaching Miracles Healings Helps Administrations Tongues	Apostleship Prophecy Teaching Miracles Healings Tongues Interpretation of tongues
Romans 12:6–8	Ephesians 4:11	1 Peter 4:11
Prophecy Serving Teaching Exhortation Giving Leading Showing mercy	Apostleship Prophecy Evangelism Pastor-Teacher	Speaking Serving

V. Is It True That Every Member of Christ's Body Has a Spiritual Gift?

When the Holy Spirit indwells us at salvation, He brings with Him the gift or gifts designed for each one of us.[7]

> But to *each one* is given the manifestation of the Spirit for the common good. . . . But one and the same Spirit works all these things, distributing to *each one* individually just as He wills. . . . But now God has placed the members, *each one* of them, in the body, just as He desired. (1 Cor. 12:7, 11, 18, emphasis added)

VI. Can Spiritual Gifts Ever Be Lost?

Although spiritual gifts can be neglected or abused, they cannot be lost, "for the gifts and the calling of God are irrevocable" (Rom. 11:29). The context of Romans 11 is not dealing with spiritual gifts but with

---

7. See also the chapter "All God's Children Have Gifts" in *Body Life*, by Ray C. Stedman, foreword by Billy Graham, 2d. ed. (Glendale, Calif.: Regal Books, 1977), pp. 38–52.

Israel. However, Paul seems to be giving us a divine principle. Like our salvation, the gifts of the Spirit are not subject to recall.

VII. How Do We Discover Which Gifts We Have?

The first step is to be *informed*. Research the gifts to know the parameters of each one. Second, be *open*. Don't be too quick to zero in on one gift to the exclusion of another. Third, be *available*. Be willing to be used by God in different areas of ministry even though you feel you're not quite ready for that task. Fourth, be *sensitive*. Carefully evaluate the effect your gifts have on others. Finally, be *sensible*. Don't force yourself to fit into a certain gift if it doesn't appear to be the one given to you.[8]

VIII. Suppose We Do Not Exercise Our Spiritual Gifts?

Exercising our gifts is a matter of obedience. "And since we have gifts that differ according to the grace given to us, let each exercise them accordingly" (Rom. 12:6a). Failure to exercise our gifts can adversely affect the Body of Christ and the very glory of God.

> As each one has received a special gift, employ it in serving one another, as good stewards of the manifold grace of God. Whoever speaks, let him speak, as it were, the utterances of God; whoever serves, let him do so as by the strength which God supplies; so that in all things God may be glorified through Jesus Christ, to whom belongs the glory and dominion forever and ever. Amen. (1 Pet. 4:10–11)

A Concluding Thought

If you're a believer in Christ, it is your responsibility as a faithful steward and a fellow laborer in the ministry to discover and develop your gifts. If you're not a believer, your greatest gift is still waiting for you under the tree, wrapped in swaddling clothes, lying in a manger (John 3:16).

 Living Insights

Study One ■■

Of all the chapters in Scripture dealing with spiritual gifts, none is more detailed than 1 Corinthians 12. Let's spend some time becoming better acquainted with this passage.

Continued on next page

8. See also the chapter titled "The Discovery of Your Gift" in McRae's book *Dynamics of Spiritual Gifts,* pp. 103–19.

- One of the finest skills you can bring to your personal Bible study is the art of asking questions. Like pry bars, strategically worded questions can give you the leverage to move hard-to-budge interpretive mountains and allow you to uncover the true meanings in God's Word. Copy the following chart into your notebook. Read through 1 Corinthians 12. Then examine this section one verse at a time and, under the appropriate headings, jot down any questions that come to your mind.

1 Corinthians 12						
Verses	Who?	What?	Where?	When?	Why?	How?

 Living Insights

Study Two

We've covered a lot of important ground in our initial study of spiritual gifts. To review this vital material, think through the following questions and write the answers in your notebook.

- What is your definition of spiritual gifts?
- What is the role of the Holy Spirit in relation to spiritual gifts?
- What are your spiritual gifts? How did you discover them?
- What advice would you give believers who have not yet discovered their gifts?
- How do your gifts help you relate to others within the Body of Christ?

Gifts That Support the Body

1 Corinthians 12:28–31

In the previous lesson we answered some basic questions about spiritual gifts. Now we'll explore Paul's metaphorical pictures of the Church as a body and as a building. Ray Stedman further illustrates these pictures in his book *Body Life.*

> He likens it to a human body of flesh and bones, made up of many members articulated and coordinated together. He also likens it to a building which he describes as growing through the centuries to be a habitation for God through the Spirit.... When Paul speaks of the church as a body he makes clear that no one joins that body except by a new birth, through faith in Jesus Christ. There is no other way into this body. Once he has become a part of that body, every member has a contribution to make. As each member works at what God has given him to do, the whole body functions as intended. When Paul describes the church as a building he makes clear that it is a living, growing building. Every Christian is a stone added to that building, a "living stone" as Peter calls him in his first letter. Each is a vital part of the great temple which the Holy Spirit is building as a habitation for God. We can never understand the church till we accept that picture.[1]

I. Clarifying the Categories of Gifts

Spiritual gifts fall naturally into three categories: support gifts, service gifts, and sign gifts. The following chart helps to sort them.

Support Gifts	Service Gifts	Sign Gifts
Apostleship	Administrations	Distinguishing of spirits
Prophecy	Exhortation	Miracles
Evangelism	Faith	Healings
Pastor-Teacher	Giving	Tongues
Teaching	Helps	Interpretation of tongues
	Showing mercy	

During this study, we'll examine the specific functions of the *support gifts,* referred to as the "greater" gifts in 1 Corinthians 12:31a.

> And God has appointed in the church, first apostles, second prophets, third teachers, then miracles, then gifts of healings, helps, administrations, various kinds of tongues. All are not apostles, are they? All are not prophets, are they?

1. Ray C. Stedman, *Body Life,* foreword by Billy Graham, 2d. ed. (Glendale, Calif.: Regal Books, 1977), pp. 70–71.

All are not teachers, are they? All are not workers of miracles, are they? All do not have gifts of healings, do they? All do not speak with tongues, do they? All do not interpret, do they? But earnestly desire the *greater* gifts. (vv. 28–31a, emphasis added)

Paul complements this list in Ephesians 4:11–12.

And He gave some as apostles, and some as prophets, and some as evangelists, and some as pastors and teachers, for the equipping of the saints for the work of service, to the building up of the body of Christ.

These gifts are public in nature and revolve around the ministry of the Word in equipping the saints for service. The *service gifts,* on the other hand, function within the body in a much more private manner. People with these gifts take on the personal ministry of encouraging, building up, and strengthening the body. Finally, the *sign gifts* are supernatural manifestations of the Spirit's power. They authenticated God's message and His messengers when the Church, in its infancy, had no completed Bible to guide and instruct its members (Heb. 2:1–4). In summary, the support gifts *equip;* the service gifts *encourage;* the sign gifts *establish.*

II. Understanding the Support Gifts

The human body contains four major systems that support and sustain our physical life: skeletal, neuromuscular, digestive, and circulatory. Our entire body is dependent on these systems. In a unique way, they correspond to the major support ministries within the Body of Christ. To change the metaphor, these gifts are the foundations and pillars that support the church. We can visualize the relationship of the support gifts to the body through the following illustration.

Gifts That Support the Body
Ephesians 4:11–12

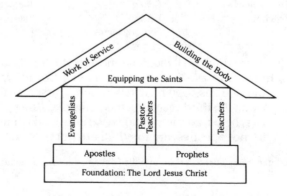

8

┌─ *Some Personal Application* ───────────────────────
Christ is both the cornerstone of the Church and the head of the Body. All power and authority are derived from Him. Apart from Christ, the Body is palsied and paralytic. Apart from His firm and even foundation, the church rests on unstable ground. If Christ's words are true on an individual level—"apart from Me you can do nothing" (John 15:5b)—they are even more true on a collective level, as a church. As a member of a local body of believers, take a look at the stature and structure of your church. Is Christ the head? Is He the foundation? Don't confuse the church's founders with the foundation, the head of the board with the head of the body, or the church constitution with the words of Christ.

A. **Apostleship** (Eph. 4:11, 1 Cor. 12:28). The skeletal system provides the body's basic support, making mobility and activity possible. Without it, the body would be only an amorphous mass of organs and muscles. The work of the apostles corresponds closely to the skeleton's function of providing a sturdy framework for the body. In a technical sense, only one who had accompanied Jesus during His earthly ministry and had personally witnessed the Resurrection was qualified to be an apostle. The choosing of Matthias as Judas's successor is a case in point (Acts 1:21–26). Paul's apostleship, like that of the original twelve disciples, was obtained by a direct commission from the Lord (compare Acts 1:1–8 with 9:1–22; see also 1 Cor. 9:1). An apostle had virtually absolute authority in the early church, and his ministry of instruction was authenticated by signs and wonders. In a nontechnical sense, the word *apostle* means merely "one who is sent." The New Testament does seem to distinguish between the technical and nontechnical usage by translating the Greek word *apostolos* in one context as "*apostles* of Jesus Christ" and in another as "*messengers* of the churches" (1 Cor. 1:1 and 2 Cor. 8:23, respectively, emphasis added). The apostle's ministry was foundational to the establishment of the Church (Eph. 2:20) and appears to have been given only during those early groundbreaking days.

B. **Prophecy** (Rom. 12:6; 1 Cor. 12:10, 14:1–40; Eph. 4:11). Closely tied to the skeletal system is the neuromuscular system. The central nervous system originates in the brain and runs down the spinal column through a network of nerve endings which weave their way through the various muscles. The brain stimulates these muscles to act and react by sending specific messages through the nerves to every part of the body. The equivalent

in the Body of Christ was the prophet. He was God's spokesman—
an infallible messenger speaking on God's behalf. This gift was
essential during the foundational stage of the Church in providing necessary instruction until the blueprint of His Word was
completed. Along with the gift of apostleship, Charles Ryrie
classifies prophecy as temporary in nature:

> The gift of prophecy included receiving a message
> directly from God through special revelation, being
> guided in declaring it to the people, and having it
> authenticated in some way by God Himself. . . . This
> too was a gift limited in its need and use, for it was
> needed during the writing of the New Testament and
> its usefulness ceased when the books were com-
> pleted.[2]

C. Evangelism (Eph. 4:11). This gift corresponds to the body's
digestive system, which takes dead food and transforms it into
a living part of the body. The only place this gift is mentioned
is in Ephesians. The term *evangelist* means "gospelizer"—one
who declares good news. It refers to one who has a unique ability to share the gospel of salvation with ease, courage, and effectiveness. Philip is called "the evangelist" in Acts 21:8, and it is
implied in 18:28 that Apollos was a gifted evangelist.

D. Pastor-Teacher (Eph. 4:11). This gift parallels the circulatory
system. In the human body, miles of veins and arteries are
routed to and from the heart. With each pump of the heart, oxy-
gen and food are distributed throughout the body while waste
products are simultaneously removed. Essentially, this is the
function of the pastor-teacher, as the heart of the local ministry.
He nourishes and protects. Like a shepherd, he leads his sheep
into green pastures beside quiet waters and watches over them
with his rod and staff to protect them from harm (Acts 20:28–29,
1 Pet. 5:1–8).

E. Teaching (1 Cor. 12:28). Cousin to the pastor-teacher gift is the
gift of teaching. The former is a guardian of the *flock* while the
latter is a guardian of the *truth*. What the professor is to the university, the teacher is to the church. Unlike the prophet, the
teacher originates nothing new; he merely defines, describes, and
declares existing revelation. Probably the most gifted teacher in
our era was C. S. Lewis, who skillfully made eternal truths vividly
clear and understandable. Although he had no local flock to
shepherd, his lifetime of refining truth continues to nourish millions around the world.

---

2. Charles Caldwell Ryrie, *The Holy Spirit* (Chicago, Ill.: Moody Press, 1970), p. 86. For uses
of the gift of prophecy in the New Testament, see Acts 11:27–28, 13:1, 21:9, and 1 Corinthians 14.

A Final Application

The Bible not only talks about the role of the support gifts but also speaks of the church's responsibility to those so gifted. The church is to follow the leadership of those with support gifts (1 Tim. 4:12–14a; Heb. 13:7, 17). It is also to honor and financially provide for those who spend their time cultivating and implementing the support gifts (1 Tim. 5:17–18). Whom are you following? If your leaders are worthy to be followed, they are worthy of your honor and support (Gal. 6:6).

 Living Insights

Study One ▬▬▬▬▬▬▬▬▬▬▬▬▬▬▬▬▬▬▬▬▬▬▬▬▬▬▬

The most public of the support gifts is the role of pastor-teacher. Let's look at some of the pastoral Epistles to learn more about this vital gift.

● Copy the following chart into your notebook and read 1 and 2 Timothy. Write down essential qualities for a pastor. Next, discern whether each quality is God-given or personally developed, and check (√) the appropriate column.

Pastoral Essentials: 1 and 2 Timothy			
Verses	Qualities	God-Given (√)	Personally Developed (√)

 Living Insights

Study Two ▬▬▬▬▬▬▬▬▬▬▬▬▬▬▬▬▬▬▬▬▬▬▬▬▬▬▬

We're using our Living Insights to focus on the gift of pastor-teacher. Let's continue to make our study even more personal. Carefully think through and answer each of the following questions.

● What is your relationship to your pastor?
● What are the strengths of the relationship?
● What are the weaknesses?
● How could you improve it?
● How could your pastor make it better?
● What can you do this week to let your pastor know that you appreciate his ministry?

11

Gifts That Serve the Body
Romans 12:1–8

An evening at the symphony. The cacophony of instruments warming up mingles with the bustling audience as ushers escort the people to their seats. The houselights slowly dim, and a hush falls over the audience. Greeted by applause, the dignified conductor ascends the podium, bows modestly, then turns to face the orchestra. A pin-drop silence settles reverently in the hall. The maestro taps the delicate baton on the music stand. The musicians raise their instruments in unisoned response.

With a dramatic sweep of the conductor's hand, the woodwind, string, brass, and percussion instruments all join to play their parts—regardless how great or how small, whether it's the crashing cymbals or the soft tiptoe of the flute. And Beethoven's Ninth Symphony becomes incarnate once again.

The soul of the audience soars, its pinions uplifted in the wake of the symphony's thundering storm. After a volley of ovations, the conductor and orchestra take their bows. The evening at the symphony is over.

Comments are rapturously exchanged in the exit aisles about the orchestra, about the conductor, about Beethoven. Visibly and audibly, they are in the forefront of our minds. What we don't notice, however, is what takes place behind the scenes—out of the public eye. We give little thought to all those people who serve diligently yet quietly in the background: ticket takers, ushers, lighting experts, stage crew. They serve in ancillary positions, silently, unobtrusively, so the audience may experience Beethoven without interruption or obstruction.

In a similar way, gifts that serve the Body of Christ operate behind the scenes. Contrary to the support gifts, which, like the conductor and orchestra, are more public in nature, the service gifts usually function offstage, out of the limelight, and far from the applause.

I. Understanding the Service Gifts

Introducing the subject of spiritual gifts in Romans 12, Paul issues a call to commitment in verse 1 coupled with a caution in verses 2 and 3.

> I urge you therefore, brethren, by the mercies of God, to present your bodies a living and holy sacrifice, acceptable to God, which is your spiritual service of worship. And do not be conformed to this world, but be transformed by the renewing of your mind, that you may prove what the will of God is, that which is good and acceptable and perfect. For through the grace given to me I say to every man among you not to think more highly of himself than he ought to think; but to think so as to have sound judgment, as God has allotted to each a measure of faith.

12

We should be aware of two crippling dangers in living the spiritual life: the world and self. With regard to the former, Paul warns *not to be conformed;* to the latter, *not to be conceited.* If we are to make an impact on the world, the world must not make an impact on us. To prevent the pressure of the world from squeezing us into its mold, we must be transformed. Our minds must be renewed. And one result of a renewed mind is viewing ourselves in proper perspective, with neither a too-high nor too-low estimation of ourselves. There is both a humility (1 Cor. 12:12–21) and a dignity (vv. 22–27) that comes with being a member of Christ's Body. Verses 4 and 5 of Romans 12 illustrate how we fit in the Body of Christ and provide us with that renewed perspective of sound judgment.

> For just as we have many members in one body and all the members do not have the same function, so we, who are many, are one body in Christ, and individually members one of another.

Since there is such a differentiation within the Body and such a dependence among its members, Paul directs us to develop and deploy our gifts in verses 6 and 8.

> And since we have gifts that differ according to the grace given to us, let each exercise them accordingly: if prophecy, according to the proportion of his faith; if service, in his serving; or he who teaches, in his teaching; or he who exhorts, in his exhortation; he who gives, with liberality; he who leads, with diligence; he who shows mercy, with cheerfulness.

Solo or Symphony

Imagine listening to a drum solo for two hours without the rest of the orchestra ever playing a note or seventy-six trombones without the rest of the marching band. As instruments were designed to blend with other instruments, so gifts within the Body of Christ were designed to mix with other complementary gifts. God orchestrated His Body to be a symphony—not a one-man band.

II. Defining the Service Gifts

In this lesson we will focus on the gifts of administration, exhortation, and faith; in the next lesson we will study three other service gifts.

  A. Administration (Rom. 12:8). We tend to equate administration with paperwork, secretarial duties, and committee meetings. This gift, however, is more comparable to the position of chief executive officer rather than secretary. Visionary . . . goal-oriented

... decisive—these words describe the person with this gift. In this passage, the Greek word is translated *lead*.[1] In 1 Corinthians 12:28 another Greek word is used, translated *administrations*,[2] but the gift is probably the same. The word used in 1 Corinthians paints a colorful picture of the person with this gift. The word means "helmsman," or "one who steers a ship." This individual was responsible for guiding a boat through stormy weather, around rocks and reefs, and into a safe harbor. The term described one who was calm, clear-thinking, and practical. From this information we can conclude that the person with the gift of administration has the ability to steer committees, entire churches, or global ministries—to keep them on course, on schedule, and off the rocks. Examples of individuals with this gift are Titus (Titus 1:5) and Timothy (1 Cor. 4:17, Phil. 2:19).

The Gift of Orchestration

Every symphony needs an arranger to orchestrate music that utilizes every instrument—from the delicate cry of the violin to the dominating thunder of the timpani. The gift of administration within the Body of Christ is there to make sure we are all in our proper place, on the same page of music, and properly cued. If you're responsible for organizing a group of people and the orchestration just isn't coming together, maybe your gift is out of position. You might be a first-chair violinist, but that doesn't necessarily make you the best arranger.

B. Exhortation (Rom. 12:8). The term means "to call alongside" with the intent of helping.[3] The person with this gift encourages others and has the ability to drive home specific truths of Scripture in such a way as to motivate application. Proverbs 25:11 describes the skill of an exhorter:

---

1. The Greek word is *proistēmi*, which literally means "to stand before." It is used of one who presides over or rules an assembly. The King James Version translates the word in this passage as "he that ruleth." See also 1 Thessalonians 5:12, where the Greek word is translated differently but has that same sense.

2. The Greek word is *kubernēsis* and means "administrations." It comes from the verb *kubernaō*, meaning "to steer." A *kubernētēs* is a "steersman, pilot, or shipmaster."

3. The Greek word is *paraklētos*. The first half of the word we know from our word *parallel*, which refers to "something placed alongside another." The second half means "to call." The Romans translated this word literally into Latin; thus, we have the word *advocate*. In German and French this word has become a common name for a lawyer—one who is called to your side to help. The same word is used to describe the Holy Spirit's ministry in John 14:16, 26; 15:26; and 16:7. He is called alongside the believer to help and to comfort in Christ's absence.

Like apples of gold in settings of silver
Is a word spoken in right circumstances.

Even when the words are firm and forthright, an exhorter comes across as a friend. This person has the ability to tell you the truth about yourself, yet with a comforting arm around your shoulder. Proverbs 27:5–6 paints a warm picture of this type of person:

Better is open rebuke
Than love that is concealed.
Faithful are the wounds of a friend,
But deceitful are the kisses of an enemy.

Two people who had the gift of exhortation were Priscilla and Aquila (Acts 18:24–28). Another person with this gift was Barnabas. In fact, his name means "Son of Encouragement" (Acts 4:36). Like so many biblical characters, Barnabas was true to his name. He came to Paul's side to comfort him when all the disciples in Jerusalem shunned him (9:26–27). And later, when Paul rejected John Mark, Barnabas was there to pick up the shattered young man and glue the pieces of his life back together so he would be useful for service once again (compare Acts 15:39 with 2 Tim. 4:11).

C. **Faith** (1 Cor. 12:9). In 1 Corinthians 12, Paul lists faith as one of the spiritual gifts. While each Christian is to be a person of faith, some have a unique ability to trust God even in the midst of overwhelming circumstances. They live their lives on the cutting edge of faith with such daring trust that their lives would not make sense if God did not exist. They are "Hebrews 11 people"— living monuments of faith—enigmas to the world but examples of encouragement to the church. A biblical example of a person with this gift is Stephen (Acts 6:5). Hudson Taylor, the missionary to China whose vision and faithfulness formed the fruitful China Inland Mission, is a more recent example.

A Final Note

Just as many different instruments make up an orchestra, so many diverse gifts make up the Body of Christ. God composed the Body so this diversity would produce a mutual dependence among the individual members (1 Cor. 12:12–27). In turn, this interdependence should foster unity (v. 25). But the world will never hear the beautiful music of Christ incarnated in the Church unless the harmony of love accompanies it. Without it, the Church is not a symphony but only a discordant collection of noisy gongs and clanging cymbals (13:1). What kind of music are you making in your church? Is it in harmony with the rest of the body?

> Is the melody one that stimulates people to sing along, or does it grate against their ears?

Living Insights

Study One ━━━━━━━━━━━━━━━━━━━━━━━━━━

This study focused on the service gifts of administration, exhortation, and faith. In preparation, we looked at the first eight verses of Romans 12; now let's dig a little deeper into this passage.

- An excellent method for gleaning further meaning from a Scripture passage is to paraphrase the text. As you write out Romans 12:1–8, try to draw the emotion and full meaning from each phrase. Make this passage come alive!

Living Insights

Study Two ━━━━━━━━━━━━━━━━━━━━━━━━━━

Have you observed the gifts of administration, exhortation, and faith in your local fellowship? Do you provide one of these gifts in the body? Can you see how these three gifts help the body run smoothly?

- Write down the name of someone in your fellowship with the gift of administration. How does this gift aid the body? What would your group be like without this person? Give some specific examples.
- Whom do you know with the gift of exhortation? Do you like being around that person? Give reasons for your answer and include concrete illustrations.
- What is the difference between the faith all believers should have and the gift of faith? Have you seen this gift in action? Describe the situation that comes to mind.

Three Quiet but Essential Gifts

Selected Scripture

Mountain climbing takes teamwork. Everest is never climbed by one man alone. Its peak is always scaled by a team. Well-trained and umbilically tied to each other by ropes, mountaineers depend not only on each other but also on their equipment.

Like guardian angels, the equipment surrounding these adventurers allows them to ascend the sheerest of peaks. Hemp ropes. Ice axes. Crampons for their boots with long metal spikes to grip the frozen ice walls.

Without these quiet but essential pieces of equipment, the mountain climbers might as well stay in the lodge, drink hot cocoa by the fireplace, and tell stories of the mountain. Without the necessary gear, it would be foolhardy if they attempted to conquer the mountain.

Similarly, within the Body of Christ are three quiet but essential gifts which help us gain secure footholds on the icy, dangerous cliffs that sometimes confront us in life. And when we slip, these gifts are the strong ropes that keep us from a deathly fall.

I. Flash versus Faith

When Paul brought the gospel to Corinth, his presentation wasn't flashy. It wasn't clothed in trendy theological terminology or fashionable rhetoric. Like a serious mountain climber, Paul wasn't interested in making a big impression at the lodge. His goal was the mountain. Consequently, his faith rested in his equipment—the internal power of the Spirit—rather than in any external human display.

> And when I came to you, brethren, I did not come with superiority of speech or of wisdom, proclaiming to you the testimony of God. For I determined to know nothing among you except Jesus Christ, and Him crucified. And I was with you in weakness and in fear and in much trembling. And my message and my preaching were not in persuasive words of wisdom, but in demonstration of the Spirit and of power, that your faith should not rest on the wisdom of men but on the power of God. (1 Cor. 2:1–5)

But the Corinthians were caught up with designer preachers ... with labels ... with the seasonal glitz of religious fashion.

> And I, brethren, could not speak to you as to spiritual men, but as to men of flesh, as to babes in Christ. I gave you milk to drink, not solid food; for you were not yet able to receive it. Indeed, even now you are not yet able, for you are still fleshly. For since there is jealousy and strife among you, are you not fleshly, and are you not

walking like mere men? For when one says, "I am of Paul," and another, "I am of Apollos," are you not mere men? (3:1–4)

Like the fashion world rallies around its Calvin Kleins and Pierre Cardins, the Corinthians rallied around Paul and Apollos. To correct this, Paul tried to get them to see beyond the designer labels and into the true fabric of the ministry.

What then is Apollos? And what is Paul? Servants through whom you believed, even as the Lord gave opportunity to each one. I planted, Apollos watered, but God was causing the growth. (vv. 5–6)

II. Three Gifts of Service

The gifts of service are not public in orientation but private. They operate quietly, yet they are the lifelines of the ministry.

A. Giving (Rom. 12:6–8). This gift is the ability to be sensitive to and to provide for the needs of the saints with great joy and generosity. In his letter to the Romans, Paul exhorted the one with the gift of giving to exercise that gift "with liberality."

And since we have gifts that differ according to the grace given to us, let each exercise them accordingly: if prophecy, according to the proportion of his faith; if service, in his serving; or he who teaches, in his teaching; or he who exhorts, in his exhortation; he who gives, with liberality; he who leads, with diligence; he who shows mercy, with cheerfulness.

All those in Christ's Body are encouraged and expected to give consistently (1 Cor. 16:2), liberally (2 Cor. 9:6), sacrificially (8:3), and cheerfully (9:7). The person with the *gift* of giving, however, has a special God-given capacity to give, an inner drive, and a longing to provide for the needs of the saints. Dorcas was a woman who appeared to have this gift. In her life we see the consistent and predominant exercise of giving.

Now in Joppa there was a certain disciple named Tabitha (which translated in Greek is called Dorcas); this woman was abounding with deeds of kindness and charity, which she continually did. (Acts 9:36)

A Precept and a Portrait

In the Sermon on the Mount, Jesus provided us with an important precept for giving.

"When therefore you give alms, do not sound a trumpet before you, as the hypocrites do in the synagogues and in the streets, that they may be honored by men. Truly I say to you, they

18

have their reward in full. But when you give alms, do not let your left hand know what your right hand is doing that your alms may be in secret; and your Father who sees in secret will repay you." (Matt. 6:2–4)

Giving, like praying (vv. 5–15), is an intimate expression of worship. And like our prayers, it can center on us rather than on the Lord. We can easily use it to further *our* glory rather than His. One way to guard against this is to make sure our giving is a private, intimate act—not a public display. In Mark 12:41–44, a portrait to rival the Mona Lisa is framed for us—the portrait of a beautiful giver.

> And He sat down opposite the treasury, and began observing how the multitude were putting money into the treasury; and many rich people were putting in large sums. And a poor widow came and put in two small copper coins, which amount to a cent. And calling His disciples to Him, He said to them, "Truly I say to you, this poor widow put in more than all the contributors to the treasury; for they all put in out of their surplus, but she, out of her poverty, put in all she owned, all she had to live on."

Is your giving like that of the hypocrites in Matthew 6—a public act of self-glorification? Or is it like that of the widow in Mark 12—a private, intimate act of worship?

B. Helping (Rom. 12:7). Serving is the ability to assist and support others in the family of God in practical ways with great faithfulness and delight. The Greek word is *diakonos,* which is translated "deacon." It means "to care for" or "to wait upon." In Acts 6:1–2, it is used of serving food or waiting on tables. In Romans 16:1, the word described Phoebe, referring to her as a "servant of the church." In Paul's list of spiritual gifts in 1 Corinthians 12:28, the word *helps* is used as a synonym for serving. It is derived from the verb in Acts 20:35.

> "In everything I showed you that by working hard in this manner you must *help* the weak and remember the words of the Lord Jesus, that He Himself said, 'It is more blessed to give than to receive.' " (emphasis added)

The household of Onesiphorus, who refreshed Paul, illustrated this gift (2 Tim. 1:16), as well as Phoebe (Rom. 16:1–2).

Servanthood doesn't come naturally to any of us. We usually want to be the one served, not the one serving. We want to be seated at the place of honor at the banquet, not given the lowly task of washing feet. We want to be exalted, not humiliated. God wants us to be exalted, too, but His path to glory and greatness takes us on the detour of a paradox: "Whoever wishes to become great among you shall be your servant; and whoever wishes to be first among you shall be slave of all. For even the Son of Man did not come to be served, but to serve, and to give His life a ransom for many" (Mark 10:43b–45). When we serve—humbly and sacrificially—we are most like the Savior, who "emptied Himself, taking the form of a bond-servant, and being made in the likeness of men" (Phil. 2:7). Invariably, the role of the servant follows the road to the cross—where self is crucified. "And being found in appearance as a man, He humbled Himself by becoming obedient to the point of death, even death on a cross" (v. 8).

C. Showing mercy (Rom. 12:8). The word *mercy* means "pity" or "compassion." It is the ability to empathize with the needs, pains, heartaches, disappointments, and sorrows of others and to be an agent of healing and restoration. People with this gift have the unique quality of emotionally identifying with the one in need. That person can "weep with those who weep" (v. 15) and "remember the prisoners, as though in prison with them" (Heb. 13:3a). Barnabas (Acts 9:26–27, 15:36–39) and Epaphroditus (Phil. 2:25–30) are two individuals who seemed to possess this important gift. But probably no one except Christ illustrated it as clearly as the Good Samaritan.

"A certain man was going down from Jerusalem to Jericho; and he fell among robbers, and they stripped him and beat him, and went off leaving him half dead. And by chance a certain priest was going down on that road, and when he saw him, he passed by on the other side. And likewise a Levite also, when he came to the place and saw him, passed by on the other side. But a certain Samaritan, who was on a journey, came upon him; and when he saw him, he felt compassion, and came to him, and bandaged up his wounds, pouring oil and wine on them; and he put him on his own beast, and brought him to an inn, and took care of him. And on the next day he took out two denarii and gave them to the innkeeper and said, 'Take care of him; and whatever more you spend, when I return, I will repay you.' Which of these three do you think proved to be a neighbor to the man who fell into the robbers' hands?" And he said, "The one who showed mercy toward him." And Jesus said to him, "Go and do the same." (Luke 10:30b–37)

A Parting Thought on Mercy

The quality of mercy is not strain'd,
It droppeth as the gentle rain from heaven
Upon the place beneath: it is twice blest;
It blesseth him that gives and him that takes.

(Shakespeare, *The Merchant of Venice*, act 4, scene 1)

 Living Insights

Study One

The gifts we explored in this study aren't crowd-oriented, but they do point us to God's glory in the working of His Body. Giving, helping, and showing mercy are *essential.*

- Copy the following chart into your notebook. Consult a concordance for the words *gave, give, help,* and *mercy.* Look up the references in your Bible and jot down a brief summary of the descriptions given in each verse. In each instance, try to discern whether the situation is the work of God or man. Check (✓) the appropriate column.

Giving, Helping, and Showing Mercy				
Words	Verses	Summaries	God's Work (✓)	Man's Work (✓)

Continued on next page

Living Insights

Giving, helping, and showing mercy are three gifts easily overlooked. Do you sometimes find yourself doing this very thing? Let's remedy the situation.

- Try to think of someone who has one of these quiet gifts. Let that person know you appreciate their contribution to the body. Use your own creativity to say thanks. A note, a phone call, a small gift, a meal, an embrace . . . you decide.

Miracles, Healings, and Tongues Today

1 Corinthians 12, 14

In ancient Rome, prominent citizens wore signet rings that bore their initials, insignia, or some other identifying inscription. They were used to press an imprint into clay or sealing wax. During this era, letters were generally written on papyrus, the precursor to paper. "The method of sealing a papyrus document was to roll it into a tube, tie a strand or cord around the centre, and seal a clay lump over the knot."[1] The imprint of the signet ring was a sign of authority. It could confirm treaties, validate commercial transactions, or authenticate the commands of an official letter. That is why the returning of the Prodigal Son's ring by his father was such a significant part of the story (Luke 15:22). In doing so, the father was restoring his son to a position of full authority.

The sign gifts in the Body of Christ functioned in a similar capacity. They were God's signet ring, which authenticated both His message and His message bearers.

I. Understanding the Term *Sign*

In previous lessons, we studied the support and service gifts. The last category of gifts we will study is the sign gifts.[2] In his gospel, John indicates that Jesus performed many signs and miracles, which verified the authenticity of who He was and what He said.

> Many other signs therefore Jesus also performed in the presence of the disciples, which are not written in this book; but these have been written that you may believe that Jesus is the Christ, the Son of God; and that believing you may have life in His name. (20:30–31)

John chose to include in his gospel only those signs that would best arouse belief in his readers. At Jesus' birth, a sign was used to distinguish the Christ Child from the other children in Bethlehem.

> "And this will be a sign for you: you will find a baby wrapped in cloths, and lying in a manger." (Luke 2:12)

Later, Paul spoke of the miraculous display of God's power as the distinguishing characteristic that proved his apostleship.

---

1. *Encyclopaedia Britannica,* 15th ed., s.v. "Seals in antiquity."

2. The Greek word for sign is *sēmeion.* It is from the root *sēma,* meaning "mark" or "characteristic." The word is used of that which distinguished a person or thing from others (Matt. 26:48, Rom. 4:11). It is used of Paul's autograph attesting the authenticity of his letters (2 Thess. 3:17) and of miraculous acts as tokens of divine authority and power (Matt. 12:38, 39; John 2:11). In the Septuagint, the Greek translation of the Old Testament, *sēmeion* is used to describe the distinguishing mark, or "sign," that the Lord put on Cain to prevent others from slaying him (Gen. 4:15).

The signs of a true apostle were performed among you with all perseverance, by signs and wonders and miracles. (2 Cor. 12:12)

The purpose of signs, therefore, was to distinguish a person as a bona fide messenger of God and to authenticate the message that person brought to the people. In the first century, when the New Testament was in the process of being completed, it was necessary for the Church to receive special revelation from God. God bridged this transitional period with several gifts that functioned as temporary conduits of His truth. Those with the gifts of apostleship, prophecy, the word of wisdom, and the word of knowledge met this need.[3] To authenticate these messages and messengers, God validated them through signs, wonders, miracles, and healings.

II. Understanding the Sign Gifts

The sign gifts are listed in 1 Corinthians 12.

To another the effecting of miracles, and to another prophecy, and to another the distinguishing of spirits, to another various kinds of tongues, and to another the interpretation of tongues.... And God has appointed in the church, first apostles, second prophets, third teachers, then miracles, then gifts of healings, helps, administrations, various kinds of tongues. (vv. 10, 28)

A. **Miracles.** The first sign gift we encounter is the gift of miracles. This is the supernatural ability to alter the laws of nature. A person with this gift could perform miracles on a grand scale, as Jesus did when He walked the earth—miracles ranging anywhere from calming the sea to raising the dead. With regard to miracles, we can make three observations.

1. **God's great eras each began with a great display of miracles.** To introduce and establish a new era, God has historically used a cluster of miraculous events. Both the Old and New Covenants were thus instituted. The era of the Law was ushered in by a concentration of supernatural incidents that began with the Exodus and continued during the Israelites' forty-year trek through the wilderness. The era of grace was

---

3. The word of knowledge (*gnōsis*) and the word of wisdom (*sophia*) are both revelatory in nature. The word of knowledge is ordinary knowledge supernaturally revealed, as shown by Peter's knowledge of Ananias and Sapphira's deception in Acts 5:1–12. The word of wisdom, on the other hand, is understanding truth that is already revealed. A distinction between the two might be implied in 1 Corinthians 13:2: "If I . . . know all mysteries and all knowledge . . ." The word of knowledge, then, is a supernatural gift of information about something or someone. The word of wisdom is the ability to understand some of the more enigmatic mysteries of the how and why concerning God's truth. For further clarification, consult *You and Your Spiritual Gifts,* by Kenneth O. Gangel (Chicago, Ill.: Moody Press, 1975), pp. 47–49, 83–85.

heralded with signs, wonders, and miracles by the King of kings Himself; these signs continued through the apostolic generation. Revelation 11 says that the new era of the Tribulation will be accompanied by prophets whose authority is validated with a display of miracles.

2. **Once the eras were underway, the miracles faded.** Hebrews 2:3b–4 establishes a chronology of events that provides a clue to the duration of these miraculous events.

> After it was at the first spoken through the Lord, it was confirmed to us by those who heard, God also bearing witness with them, both by signs and wonders and by various miracles and by gifts of the Holy Spirit according to His own will.

The Lord spent more than three years imparting His teaching into the hearts and minds of the disciples. After His ascension, this privileged group was commissioned as apostles to be Christ's witnesses throughout the world (Acts 1). God used a supernatural display to confirm these men to the people. The words "with them" in verse 4 of Hebrews 2 indicate that the miracles authenticated those messengers "who heard" the actual words of the Lord; namely, the apostles. A study of church history reveals that by the end of the first century these miraculous gifts were no longer exercised.[4]

3. **Cessation of the *gift* of miracles does not mean God has ceased *giving* miracles.** Our God is a miraculous God who doesn't change (Heb. 1:10–11). His methods do, however. Throughout history there have been only three periods when miraculous events played a prominent role: the time of Moses, the time of Elijah and Elisha, and the time of Christ and the apostles. Miracles as a common experience are conspicuously absent from both Israel's and the church's history. Many of the greatest men of the Old Testament never performed a miracle, including Noah, Abraham, and David. These men, however, did see the miraculous hand of God at work in their lives and in the lives of the people around them.

B. **Healing.** This gift is the supernatural ability to instantly restore someone to mental or physical health. A person with this gift could perform the same type of healing as Christ: healing the sick, raising the dead, cleansing the lepers, and casting out demons (Matt. 10:5–8). We find one example in Acts 3:1–10.

---

4. An excellent discussion on the duration of the gifts can be found in William McRae's book *Dynamics of Spiritual Gifts* (Grand Rapids, Mich.: Zondervan Publishing House, 1976), pp. 90–99. See also 1 Corinthians 13:8–13.

Now Peter and John were going up to the temple at the ninth hour, the hour of prayer. And a certain man who had been lame from his mother's womb was being carried along, whom they used to set down every day at the gate of the temple which is called Beautiful, in order to beg alms of those who were entering the temple. And when he saw Peter and John about to go into the temple, he began asking to receive alms. And Peter, along with John, fixed his gaze upon him and said, "Look at us!" And he began to give them his attention, expecting to receive something from them. But Peter said, "I do not possess silver and gold, but what I do have I give to you: In the name of Jesus Christ the Nazarene—walk!" And seizing him by the right hand, he raised him up; and immediately his feet and his ankles were strengthened. And with a leap, he stood upright and began to walk; and he entered the temple with them, walking and leaping and praising God. And all the people saw him walking and praising God; and they were taking note of him as being the one who used to sit at the Beautiful Gate of the temple to beg alms and they were filled with wonder and amazement at what had happened to him.

A second example of this gift is found in Acts 19:11–12.

And God was performing extraordinary miracles by the hands of Paul, so that handkerchiefs or aprons were even carried from his body to the sick, and the diseases left them and the evil spirits went out.

Faith healers of today range from tent-meeting country revivalists to television celebrities. They may have large and loyal followings, but often their theology is not as tight as their tent stakes or as focused as their cameras. We need to address three claims made today concerning healing.

1. **It is asserted that healing is guaranteed in the Atonement.** This claim is based on Isaiah 53:5, which says: "by His scourging we are healed." The context of this passage, however, is not physical infirmities but spiritual ones.

But He was pierced through for our transgressions,
He was crushed for our iniquities;
The chastening for our well-being fell upon Him,
And by His scourging we are healed.
All of us like sheep have gone astray,

Each of us has turned to his own way;
But the Lord has caused the iniquity of us all
To fall on Him....
But the Lord was pleased
To crush Him, putting Him to grief;
If He would render Himself as a guilt offering,
He will see His offspring,
He will prolong His days,
And the good pleasure of the Lord will prosper
    in His hand.
As a result of the anguish of His soul,
He will see it and be satisfied;
By His knowledge the Righteous One,
My Servant, will justify the many,
As He will bear their iniquities.
    (vv. 5–6, 10–11)

The whole thrust of the Isaiah prophecy is that the Servant of the Lord (Jesus) will provide healing for our spiritual disease, which is sin. God placed our crushing iniquities on Jesus at the cross. In bearing the brunt of God's wrath for those iniquities, Jesus is able to offer us judicial acquittal in God's eyes. Peter quotes from this passage in 1 Peter 2:24–25. Again, the context is spiritual healing—not physical.

And He Himself bore our sins in His body on the cross, that we might die to sin and live to righteousness; for by His wounds you were healed. For you were continually straying like sheep, but now you have returned to the Shepherd and Guardian of your souls.

2. **It is asserted that it is God's will for every sick person to be healed.** There are no scriptural grounds on which to base this opinion. In 2 Corinthians 12:1–10, Paul asked God three times that his physical infirmity be taken from him, but his request was denied. If it is God's will that every sickness be healed, certainly He would not have withheld relief for such a man of faith as the Apostle Paul. Yet God does use sickness and suffering to cause us to depend on Him more fully. In C. S. Lewis's words, pain is "His megaphone to rouse a deaf world."[5]

┌─ *The Redemptive Value of Sickness* ──────────────────
│ "I am progressing along the path of life in my ordinary
│ contentedly fallen and godless condition, absorbed in

5. C. S. Lewis, *The Problem of Pain* (New York, N.Y.: Macmillan Co., 1962), p. 93.

> a merry meeting with my friends for the morrow or a bit of work that tickles my vanity to-day, a holiday or a new book, when suddenly a stab of abdominal pain that threatens serious disease . . . sends this whole pack of cards tumbling down. At first I am overwhelmed, and all my little happinesses look like broken toys. Then, slowly and reluctantly, bit by bit, I try to bring myself into the frame of mind that I should be in at all times. I remind myself that all these toys were never intended to possess my heart, that my true good is in another world and my only real treasure is Christ."[6]

3. **It is asserted that physical illness is the result of personal sin or demonic activity.** Although at times sickness may be attributed to personal sin (1 Cor. 11:28–30) and to demonic activity (Matt. 9:32–33), it often has no direct connection to either of these (Mark 5:21–43, John 9, Mark 1:32–34). If sin were the cause of sickness, it would be logical to assume that when the sin was forgiven, we would be healed. First John 1:9 provides a wonderful promise that says if we confess our sins, we will have cleansing— but it does not say that physical healing will take place. In his discussion on how the church should meet the needs of the sick, James implies that sometimes sickness may have a causal relationship to sin, but he is very careful not to make an absolute out of that possibility (5:14–16). Does God heal today? You bet He does. James describes the biblical healing process of today.

> Is anyone among you sick? Let him call for the elders of the church, and let them pray over him, anointing him with oil in the name of the Lord. (v. 14)

The notes in the margin of the New American Standard Bible give the literal rendering of the Greek as "having anointed," indicating that the anointing takes place prior to prayer. The word *anoint* means "massage." In James's day, oil and wine were used for medicinal purposes (Luke 10:34, 1 Tim. 5:23). James is probably referring to the application of medicinal help, which in those days was frequently done by men in the church. Prayer was then offered on the sick person's behalf.

C. **Tongues.** Like the Tower of Babel, the subject of tongues has created both confusion and division. Ironically, when the gift was

---

6. Lewis, *The Problem of Pain,* p. 106.

given at Pentecost, its effect was a reversal of Babel; instead of language dividing mankind, by the gift of the Holy Spirit it united people of different nationalities.

> And when the day of Pentecost had come, they were all together in one place. And suddenly there came from heaven a noise like a violent, rushing wind, and it filled the whole house where they were sitting. And there appeared to them tongues as of fire distributing themselves, and they rested on each one of them. And they were all filled with the Holy Spirit and began to speak with other tongues, as the Spirit was giving them utterance.
>
> Now there were Jews living in Jerusalem, devout men, from every nation under heaven. And when this sound occurred, the multitude came together, and were bewildered, because they were each one hearing them speak in his own language. And they were amazed and marveled, saying, "Why, are not all these who are speaking Galileans? And how is it that we each hear them in our own language to which we were born? Parthians and Medes and Elamites, and residents of Mesopotamia, Judea and Cappadocia, Pontus and Asia, Phrygia and Pamphylia, Egypt and the districts of Libya around Cyrene, and visitors from Rome, both Jews and proselytes, Cretans and Arabs—we hear them in our own tongues speaking of the mighty deeds of God." (Acts 2:1–11)

Clearly, we can learn two things from Pentecost. First, tongues were uniquely related to the Jews (vv. 5, 10). Second, tongues communicated known languages (vv. 8, 11). In Paul's central teaching on tongues, he interprets the Pentecost experience theologically and gives some guidelines for its use within the church.

> Brethren, do not be children in your thinking; yet in evil be babes, but in your thinking be mature. In the Law it is written, "By men of strange tongues and by the lips of strangers I will speak to this people, and even so they will not listen to Me," says the Lord. So then tongues are for a sign, not to those who believe, but to unbelievers; but prophecy is for a sign, not to unbelievers, but to those who believe. (1 Cor. 14:20–22)

In verse 21, Paul quotes Isaiah 28:11. The phrase "this people" can only be interpreted contextually to refer to the Jewish nation. Paul is quoting from a passage concerning judgment upon Israel.

In doing so, he interprets the phenomenon of tongues as a sign to the unbelieving Jew (1 Cor. 14:22). The sign was a judicial rap of God's gavel upon the nation. Because they had dropped the torch by failing to witness to the nations of the world, God removed from them the privilege of being His light bearers. Instead, God passed the torch to the Gentile church. The "light of the world" would now be the Gentiles, not the Jews; the "city set on a hill" would be the church, not Jerusalem (Matt. 5:14). When the Jews heard the evangelistic message from the lips of Gentiles, it was a sign to them that, as a nation, they had forfeited their privilege and were being set aside. In 1 Corinthians 14:23–28, Paul turns his attention to how the gift should be used in a predominantly Gentile assembly.

> If therefore the whole church should assemble together and all speak in tongues, and ungifted men or unbelievers enter, will they not say that you are mad? But if all prophesy, and an unbeliever or an ungifted man enters, he is convicted by all, he is called to account by all; the secrets of his heart are disclosed; and so he will fall on his face and worship God, declaring that God is certainly among you.

> What is the outcome then, brethren? When you assemble, each one has a psalm, has a teaching, has a revelation, has a tongue, has an interpretation. Let all things be done for edification. If anyone speaks in a tongue, it should be by two or at the most three, and each in turn, and let one interpret; but if there is no interpreter, let him keep silent in the church; and let him speak to himself and to God.

His guidelines are that tongues, like all the gifts, were given for the common good. In the church, tongues were for public use, not private. They were to be used in an orderly manner to avoid confusion, and an interpreter was always to be present so the whole body might be edified.

III. Application Related to the Sign Gifts

The sign gifts were important to the Church in its infancy to establish it in a uniquely visible way, to confirm the words of the apostles, and to authenticate them as genuine messengers of God. As the Church's foundation was laid and God's Word was completed, the necessity of the sign gifts was eclipsed by the Church's growth to maturity. Today, God's self-authenticating Word bears its own testimony. In the Spirit's strong hands, it provides us with all we need to be equipped for His service.

All Scripture is inspired by God and profitable for teaching, for reproof, for correction, for training in righteousness; that the man of God may be adequate, equipped for every good work. (2 Tim. 3:16–17)

 Living Insights

Study One ▬▬▬▬▬▬▬▬▬▬▬▬▬▬▬▬▬▬▬▬▬▬▬▬▬▬▬▬▬▬▬

We have attempted to explain the sign gifts honestly and objectively. A subject this complex may take some time to sink in. Let's begin this process.

- The first gift we discussed was *miracles*. Let's concentrate our attention on that subject. Read through the lesson again and look up the corresponding passages. Do these verses cause you to agree with our conclusions? Why or why not?
- The second topic we dealt with was *healing*. Repeat the process for this gift. As you read the verses, do you concur with the points made in the lesson? Why or why not?

 Living Insights

Study Two ▬▬▬▬▬▬▬▬▬▬▬▬▬▬▬▬▬▬▬▬▬▬▬▬▬▬▬▬▬▬▬

Let's use this time to go back through the lesson and reflect specifically on the section dealing with the gift of tongues. Read 1 Corinthians 12–14 and compare it with the points in the lesson. What is your position on tongues? What questions persist in your mind? How can you answer these questions?

Guidelines for Using Your Spiritual Gifts

1 Timothy 4:11–16

James Dobson's book *The Strong-willed Child* covers childhood from birth through adolescence. He titles his eighth chapter "The Strong-willed Adolescent" and subtitles it "Is There Any Other Kind?" In the following excerpt, he humorously describes those adolescent years.

> Alas, we arrive now at the door of adolescence: that dynamic time of life which comes in with a pimple and goes out with a beard—those flirtatious years when girls begin to powder and boys begin to puff. It's an exciting phase of childhood, I suppose, but to be honest, I wouldn't want to stumble through it again. I doubt that the reader would either. We adults remember all too clearly the fears and jeers and tears that represented our own tumultuous youth. Perhaps that is why parents begin to quake and tremble when their children approach the adolescent years. (By the way, have you heard of the new wristwatch created exclusively for the anxious parents of teen-agers? After 11 P.M. it wrings its hands every fifteen minutes.)[1]

If God were human, certainly He would be pacing heaven, wringing His hands like a worried parent, wondering what His adolescent children were doing with their newfound truth about spiritual gifts. Fortunately, God is not an anxious parent. Instead of biting His nails during our adolescence, He puts His arm around us in confidence.

> Let no one look down on your youthfulness, but rather in speech, conduct, love, faith and purity, show yourself an example of those who believe. (1 Tim. 4:12)

I. Adolescent Attitudes

As we develop during our adolescent years, we find ourselves teetering shyly between childhood and adulthood—between theory and practice. During that awkward pubescent stage, our attitudes often manifest a certain arrogance and defiance. In the same way, there are four attitudes regarding spiritual gifts that we should be careful to avoid.

A. "I'll exercise my gifts when the right feeling of inspiration comes from God." Spiritual gifts aren't prefaced with tingling feelings or mountain-top moments. Notice, rather, how calmly and purposely God gives them.

---

1. James Dobson, *The Strong-willed Child* (Wheaton, Ill.: Tyndale House Publishers, 1978), pp. 189–90.

But to each one is given the manifestation of the Spirit for the common good. For to one is given the word of wisdom through the Spirit, and to another the word of knowledge according to the same Spirit; to another faith by the same Spirit, and to another gifts of healing by the one Spirit, and to another the effecting of miracles, and to another prophecy, and to another the distinguishing of spirits, to another various kinds of tongues, and to another the interpretation of tongues. But one and the same Spirit works all these things, distributing to each one individually just as He wills. (1 Cor. 12:7–11)

B. **"My gifts are the most important of all" or, conversely, "the least important."** In either of these extreme adolescent attitudes, self is the center of focus, not the Lord. Superiority and inferiority complexes have the same root: preoccupation with self. In the Body of Christ, every member is important; every gift is essential. No gift should be exalted.

For the body is not one member, but many. If the foot should say, "Because I am not a hand, I am not a part of the body," it is not for this reason any the less a part of the body. And if the ear should say, "Because I am not an eye, I am not a part of the body," it is not for this reason any the less a part of the body. If the whole body were an eye, where would the hearing be? If the whole were hearing, where would the sense of smell be? (vv. 14–17)

And no gift should be excluded.

But now there are many members, but one body. And the eye cannot say to the hand, "I have no need of you"; or again the head to the feet, "I have no need of you." On the contrary, it is much truer that the members of the body which seem to be weaker are necessary; and those members of the body, which we deem less honorable, on these we bestow more abundant honor, and our unseemly members come to have more abundant seemliness, whereas our seemly members have no need of it. But God has so composed the body, giving more abundant honor to that member which lacked, that there should be no division in the body, but that the members should have the same care for one another. (vv. 20–25)

C. **"I refuse all involvement not related to my gifts."** This statement does not reflect the attitude of a mature Christian. Although Timothy had the gift of being a pastor-teacher

(1 Tim. 4:13–14), Paul instructed him to also do the work of an evangelist (2 Tim. 4:5). Most spiritual gifts should find expression in the life of every committed believer: we should all serve, give, teach, evangelize, exhort—regardless of what our particular gifts are.

D. "I quit—ministry is too discouraging and I'm not appreciated." A person with this childish attitude wants an easy road paved with accolades and applause. But the ministry seldom offers a smooth freeway—even for the most gifted—as exemplified by Paul's experiences.

> I have fought the good fight, I have finished the course, I have kept the faith. . . . Make every effort to come to me soon; for Demas, having loved this present world, has deserted me and gone to Thessalonica; Crescens has gone to Galatia, Titus to Dalmatia. . . . Alexander the coppersmith did me much harm; the Lord will repay him according to his deeds. Be on guard against him yourself, for he vigorously opposed our teaching. At my first defense no one supported me, but all deserted me; may it not be counted against them. But the Lord stood with me, and strengthened me, in order that through me the proclamation might be fully accomplished, and that all the Gentiles might hear; and I was delivered out of the lion's mouth. (2 Tim. 4:7, 9–10, 14–17)

The ministry is often a devastating battle filled with deserters and enemies.

Attitude Exam

In his discussion of spiritual gifts in Ephesians 4, Paul tells us that "we are no longer to be children" (v. 14).

> But speaking the truth in love, we are to grow up in all aspects into Him, who is the head, even Christ, from whom the whole body, being fitted and held together by that which every joint supplies, according to the proper working of each individual part, causes the growth of the body for the building up of itself in love. (vv. 15–16)

The body will mature when each member gives up the petty quibbles of adolescence and pitches in with a spirit of selfless love. Take a minute to examine your attitudes. Are they adult or adolescent? If the latter, isn't it about time to grow up and graduate from junior high?

II. Adult Approaches

In another passage on spiritual gifts, Paul writes: "When I was a child, I used to speak as a child, think as a child, reason as a child; when I became a man, I did away with childish things" (1 Cor. 13:11). We now want to leave our adolescent attitudes behind and concentrate on developing an adult approach to using our spiritual gifts.

A. Eight words to remember. In 1 Timothy 4:14a, Paul gives Timothy eight words to remember regarding his gift: "Do not neglect the spiritual gift within you."

A Little Neglect

Proverbs 24:30–34 vividly describes how neglect can affect your life.

I passed by the field of the sluggard,
And by the vineyard of the man lacking sense;
And behold, it was completely overgrown with
thistles,
Its surface was covered with nettles,
And its stone wall was broken down.
When I saw, I reflected upon it;
I looked, and received instruction.
"A little sleep, a little slumber,
A little folding of the hands to rest,"
Then your poverty will come as a robber,
And your want like an armed man.

For the gardener, diligence produces fruitfulness; negligence produces weeds. Are you diligent with regard to your gifts ... or negligent? You don't have to be lazy for your gifts to become overgrown with thistles, just a little negligent—"a *little* sleep, a *little* slumber, a *little* folding of the hands to rest."

B. Four guidelines to follow. Preventing your gifts from becoming overgrown with neglect takes some attentive gardening. Here are some guidelines from 1 Timothy 4:11–16 to help you cultivate your gifts.

1. **Gain information.** In verse 11, Paul exhorts Timothy to "prescribe and teach these things." Nothing dispels ignorance better than information from the inspired text.

   The unfolding of Thy words gives light;
   It gives understanding to the simple. (Ps. 119:130)

   Confusing fog has enveloped this whole area of spiritual gifts, and the only way to dissipate the mist is for it to be burnt off by Scripture's dawning light.

2. **Exhibit toleration.** Next, Paul instructs Timothy to "let no one look down on your youthfulness" (v. 12). He warns Timothy against developing an inferiority complex simply because of his age. If we apply Paul's words to spiritual gifts, we should tolerate all the gifts, regardless how insignificant or lowly they seem (1 Cor. 12:21–25).

3. **Focus your attention.** Paul's counsel to Timothy continues with this bit of advice: "Until I come, give attention to the public reading of Scripture, to exhortation and teaching" (1 Tim. 4:13). Paul didn't tell Timothy to shoulder the entire work load. Rather, he was to concentrate on his specific gifts. Timothy was to quarterback the church, not be a one-man team. Similarly, God doesn't expect us to volunteer for every project, serve on every committee, and take up the slack on every responsibility. He expects us to focus our attention on our gifts and to exercise them faithfully.

4. **Seek confirmation.** Timothy is then instructed to follow certain guidelines in using his gifts: "Take pains with these things; be absorbed in them, so that your progress may be evident to all" (v. 15). Confirmation from others is an important factor in discovering and developing your gifts. As you put your gifts to work, your effectiveness should be evident to others. Their observations will confirm whether you possess those gifts. For example, if your Sunday school students crowd around you after class with questions and appreciation, that's confirmation. But if they constantly look at the clock, fidget, and file out in a wordless and hurried exit, you might want to take a red pen and put a big question mark over the gifts of teaching and exhortation.

> **A Word to Parents**
>
> Regarding confirmation, parents, no one longs for or needs your confirmation more than your children. This subject is skillfully and sensitively addressed by Gary Smalley and John Trent in their insightful book *The Blessing.* They illustrate how parental blessing, or the lack of it, affects children throughout their entire lives.

C. **Two warnings to heed.** As a final word to Timothy about his gift, Paul gives the young pastor two warnings: "Pay close attention *to yourself* and *to your teaching*" (v. 16, emphasis added). Preaching and practice have a symbiotic relationship: they are mutually dependent on each other. Teaching is only as powerful as the life behind it, and a life is only as powerful as the teaching behind it.

III. An Added Application

In the vast wastelands of West Texas is an old oil field called Yates's Pool. Back in the Great Depression, the owner of this land, Mr. Yates, was unable to pay the mortgage on his ranch. To prevent foreclosure and to feed and clothe his family, he had to apply for a government subsidy. Impoverished, Yates struggled to keep his sheep ranch solvent. During this time, a seismographic crew suspected there was oil under the property and asked for permission to drill a wildcat well. Feeling he had nothing to lose, Yates agreed. At 1,115 feet they struck oil . . . eighty thousand barrels of it . . . a day! Dozens of other wells were drilled. All struck oil, and a number of them produced more than twice the volume of the first well. In fact, thirty years after that first well was discovered, a government test showed that one of the wells still had the potential of 125,000 barrels a day. And all of that came into the hands of poor Mr. Yates. To this day, the land is worth millions of dollars. Here was a poverty-stricken man living on a government subsidy when he had the potential of being a multimillionaire—and he didn't even know it! Yates is a perfect illustration of so many Christians. It is possible for potential millionaires in the family of God to live on a subsidy and eke out a marginal existence, knowing nothing of the potential riches within them. The Lord has given each of us a well, a reservoir of untapped ability, in the form of spiritual gifts. As we conclude our study, now is the time to start drilling—to discover that vast pool of resources the Spirit has placed within you. And when your well comes in, like it did for Mr. Yates, it will forever change your life—and the lives of those around you!

Living Insights

Study One ■━━━

"Do not neglect the spiritual gift within you" (1 Tim. 4:14a). How can you avoid neglecting your gifts? We've learned some vital lessons about gifts, but what now? Let's push on!

- We presented four practical guidelines in this study. How do they apply to you and your gifts? Evaluate yourself honestly and write

Continued on next page

your answers next to each guideline in the following chart. If you feel particularly weak in one area, jot down some positive ways to improve.

How to Apply Your Spiritual Gifts	
Gain Information	
Exhibit Toleration	
Focus Your Attention	
Seek Confirmation	

 Living Insights

Study Two ▬▬▬▬▬▬▬▬▬▬▬▬▬▬▬▬▬▬▬▬▬▬▬▬▬▬▬

It's always valuable to devote some time for review when we come to the end of a study. Let's do that by paging back through our notes and completing the following exercises.

- Jot down the three most significant truths you learned in this study.
- What truth was reinforced for you as a result of studying spiritual gifts?
- List two or three changes you can make in your life concerning your spiritual gifts.

Books for Probing Further

As he concludes 1 Corinthians 12, Paul admonishes us to desire the greater gifts. However, with the words "And I show you a still more excellent way" (v. 31b), he turns our focus from the Spirit's greater gifts to His greatest fruit: *love.* Previously, Paul has compared the gifts of the Spirit to eyes, hands, and feet in the Body of Christ. In chapter 13, he reveals love to be the *heart* of that Body.

> If I speak with tongues of men and of angels, but do not have love, I have become a noisy gong or a clanging cymbal. (v. 1)

Love brings the harmonious blending of diverse instruments into a symphonic unity. Without it, we sound like spoiled children harshly pounding the ivory keys of an exquisite piano. And instead of producing heartwarming music, we give people headaches.

We can accumulate mountains of religious activity, yet without love, they're only molehills in God's eyes.

> And if I have the gift of prophecy, and know all mysteries and all knowledge; and if I have all faith, so as to remove mountains, but do not have love, I am nothing. And if I give all my possessions to feed the poor, and if I deliver my body to be burned, but do not have love, it profits me nothing. (vv. 2–3)

Love's heartbeat keeps the Body of Christ warm and alive. If the heart goes bad, it affects every area of the body and every area of our lives—every thought, every action, every relationship. Heart disease is the number one killer in America, and millions are spent each year to diagnose and treat it. Stress tests, EKGs, and angiograms test our physical hearts. But what kind of diagnostic tool can we use to test our love? In the following verses, Paul gives love the ultimate stress test.

> Love is patient, love is kind, and is not jealous; love does not brag and is not arrogant, does not act unbecomingly; it does not seek its own, is not provoked, does not take into account a wrong suffered, does not rejoice in unrighteousness, but rejoices with the truth; bears all things, believes all things, hopes all things, endures all things. Love never fails. (vv. 4–8a)

How healthy is your love according to Paul's test? Are your arteries clogged with selfishness? Is your blood pressure out of control? If so, God can replace that old, hardened heart with a new, healthy one. He can, as He did with David, create in you a clean heart (Ps. 51:10a). He can take an impatient mother and make her patient; an unkind father and make him kind; a jealous mate, trusting; an arrogant braggart, humble. He can give you a heart of love.

Changing focus again from the body's heart to its individual parts, Paul begins chapter 14 with an exhortation: "Pursue love, yet desire earnestly spiritual gifts." I hope this study on spiritual gifts has created in you a desire to discover and develop yours. We are the hands and feet of Christ—we walk this world in His absence to give it His tender and merciful touch. We can't do that very well without using our spiritual gifts . . . and we can't do it at all without love.

If indeed these studies have cultivated in you an earnest desire to discover and develop your spiritual gifts, the following books should help you in that adventure.

The Expositor's Bible Commentary, vol. 10, Frank E. Gaebelein, gen. ed. Grand Rapids, Mich.: Zondervan Publishing House, 1976. This excellent volume includes commentaries on Romans and 1 Corinthians—two books that are essential for a thorough study of spiritual gifts. The format is useful for a broad audience. The main text is an accurate, readable exegesis, while the more technical points are confined to footnotes.

Gangel, Kenneth O. *You and Your Spiritual Gifts.* Chicago, Ill.: Moody Press, 1975. This small but helpful book gives a brief introduction to spiritual gifts and then devotes a chapter apiece for the study of each individual gift. Helpful notes at the end of the book provide a wealth of cross-reference material.

Hay, Alexander Rattray. *The New Testament Order for Church and Missionary.* Audubon, N.J.: New Testament Missionary Union, n.d. This book is a study on the structure and order of the New Testament church with applications for implementing its example today. Comprehensive in scope, the book not only discusses spiritual gifts but church government, discipline, and communion as well.

McRae, William. *Dynamics of Spiritual Gifts.* Grand Rapids, Mich.: Zondervan Publishing House, 1976. This is probably the best single volume available on spiritual gifts. Topics include the definition, distribution, description, distinctions, discovery, and development of gifts. The book is well written and thoroughly researched, and it contains a number of helpful charts and notes.

Ryrie, Charles Caldwell. *The Holy Spirit.* Chicago, Ill.: Moody Press, 1970. An overview of the biblical teaching on the Holy Spirit, this succinct study includes a helpful section on spiritual gifts and also deals with the role of the Holy Spirit in relation to creation, the Bible, unbelievers, and believers.

Stedman, Ray C. *Body Life,* 2d. ed., foreword by Billy Graham. Glendale, Calif.: Regal Books, 1972. This was the first book to educate our generation on how spiritual gifts are to operate within the Body of Christ. It is based on the author's experience as pastor of the Peninsula Bible Church and on New Testament principles. The Body-Life services at Stedman's church provide us with a long-needed example of first-century Christianity at work.

Walvoord, John F. *The Holy Spirit.* Grand Rapids, Mich.: Zondervan Publishing House, 1969. An exhaustive, in-depth textbook from the former president of Dallas Theological Seminary, this valuable resource is an outgrowth of Walvoord's seminary lectures on pneumatology, the study of the Holy Spirit.

Insight for Living
Cassette Tapes
SPIRITUAL GIFTS

There could hardly be a more important message for Christians to hear than this one. You will learn what the gifts are, why God has given them, and how to know which ones you possess. This is "Body truth" every believer needs to know. When properly understood and applied, it can revolutionize your walk with Christ as well as your involvement in your local church.

			U.S.	Canadian
SPG	CS	Cassette series—includes album cover	$18.75	$23.75
		Individual cassettes—include messages A and B	5.00	6.35

These prices are effective as of January 1987 and are subject to change without notice.

SPG 1-A: *Spiritual Gifts in a Spiritual Body*
1 Corinthians 12:1–11
   B: *Gifts That Support the Body*
1 Corinthians 12:28–31

SPG 2-A: *Gifts That Serve the Body*
Romans 12:1–8
   B: *Three Quiet but Essential Gifts*
Selected Scripture

SPG 3-A: *Miracles, Healings, and Tongues Today*
1 Corinthians 12, 14
   B: *Guidelines for Using Your Spiritual Gifts*
1 Timothy 4:11–16

Ordering Information

U.S. ordering information: You are welcome to use our toll-free number (for Visa and MasterCard orders only) between the hours of 8:30 A.M. and 4:00 P.M., Pacific time, Monday through Friday. The number is **(800) 772-8888**. This number may be used anywhere in the continental United States excluding California, Hawaii, and Alaska. Orders from those areas are handled through our Sales Department at **(714) 870-9161**. We are unable to accept collect calls.

Your order will be processed promptly. We ask that you allow four to six weeks for delivery by fourth-class mail. If you wish your order to be shipped first-class, please add 10 percent of the total order cost (not including California sales tax) for shipping and handling.

Canadian ordering information: Your order will be processed promptly. We ask that you allow approximately four weeks for delivery by first-class mail to the U.S./Canadian border. All orders will be shipped from our office in Fullerton, California. For our listeners in British Columbia, a 7 percent sales tax must be added to the total of all tape orders (not including first-class postage). For further information, please contact our office at **(604) 272-5811**.

Payment options: We accept personal checks, money orders, Visa, and MasterCard in payment for materials ordered. Unfortunately, we are unable to offer invoicing or COD orders. If the amount of your check or money order is less than the amount of your purchase, your check will be returned so that you may place your order again with the correct amount. All orders must be paid in full before shipment can be made.

Returned checks: There is a $10 charge for any returned check (regardless of the amount of your order) to cover processing and invoicing.

Guarantee: Our tapes are guaranteed for ninety days against faulty performance or breakage due to a defect in the tape. For best results, please be sure your tape recorder is in good operating condition and is cleaned regularly.

Mail your order to one of the following addresses:

Insight for Living	Insight for Living Ministries
Sales Department	Post Office Box 2510
Post Office Box 4444	Vancouver, BC
Fullerton, CA 92634	Canada V6B 3W7

Quantity discounts and gift certificates are available upon request.

Overseas ordering information is provided on the reverse side of the order form.

Order Form

Please send me the following cassette tapes:

The current series: ☐ SPG CS Spiritual Gifts

Individual cassettes: ☐ SPG 1 ☐ SPG 2 ☐ SPG 3

I am enclosing:

$_____ To purchase the cassette series for $18.75 (in Canada $23.75*) which includes the album cover

$_____ To purchase individual tapes at $5.00 each (in Canada $6.35*)

$_____ Total of purchases

$_____ If the order will be delivered in California, please add 6 percent sales tax

$_____ U.S. residents please add 10 percent for first-class shipping and handling if desired

$_____ *British Columbia residents please add 7 percent sales tax

$_____ Canadian residents please add 6 percent for postage

$_____ **Overseas residents please add appropriate postage** (See postage chart under "Overseas Ordering Information.")

$_____ As a gift to the Insight for Living radio ministry for which a tax-deductible receipt will be issued

$_____ **Total amount due (Please do not send cash.)**

Form of payment:

☐ Check or money order made payable to Insight for Living

☐ Credit card (Visa or MasterCard only)

If there is a balance: ☐ apply it as a donation ☐ please refund

---

Credit card purchases:

☐ Visa ☐ MasterCard number _____

Expiration date _____

Signature _____

We cannot process your credit card purchase without your signature.

Name _____

Address _____

_____

City _____

State/Province _____ Zip/Postal code _____

Country _____

Telephone ( ) _____ Radio station ___ ___ ___ ___

Should questions arise concerning your order, we may need to contact you.

Overseas Ordering Information

If you do not live in the United States or Canada, please note the following information. This will ensure efficient processing of your request.

Estimated time of delivery: We ask that you allow approximately twelve to sixteen weeks for delivery by surface mail. If you would like your order sent airmail, the length of delivery may be reduced. All orders will be shipped from our office in Fullerton, California.

Payment options: Due to fluctuating currency rates, we can accept only personal checks made payable in U.S. funds, international money orders, Visa, and MasterCard in payment for materials ordered. If the amount of your check or money order is less than the amount of your purchase, your check will be returned so that you may place your order again with the correct amount. All orders must be paid in full before shipment can be made.

Returned checks: There is a $10 charge for any returned check (regardless of the amount of your order) to cover processing and invoicing.

Postage and handling: Please add to the amount of purchase the postage cost for the service you desire. All orders must include postage based on the chart below.

Purchase Amount		Surface Postage	Airmail Postage
From	To	Percentage of Order	Percentage of Order
$ .01	$15.00	40%	75%
15.01	75.00	25%	45%
75.01	or more	15%	40%

Guarantee: Our tapes are guaranteed for ninety days against faulty performance or breakage due to a defect in the tape. For best results, please be sure your tape recorder is in good operating condition and is cleaned regularly.

Mail your order or inquiry to the following address:

Insight for Living
Sales Department
Post Office Box 4444
Fullerton, CA 92634

Quantity discounts and gift certificates are available upon request.